The house in the tree

Story by Beverley Randell

Illustrated by Linda McClelland

Dad made a house
up in the tree
for Jessica and little Daniel.

Jessica helped Dad.
She liked climbing trees.

3

Jessica liked playing
up in the tree house.
She liked looking down
at the house and the garden
and the cows.
She saw Daniel in the garden.
"Come on, Daniel," she said.
"You come up, too."

"I can't get up,"
said Daniel.
"You come down
and help me up, Jessica.
I'm not big like you."

And he cried.

Jessica came down
and she helped
little Daniel
climb up.
"Come on.
Up you get,"
she said.

Gran saw Jessica helping Daniel.
"He is too little to climb
up to the tree house," she said.

"He likes playing with Jessica,"
said Dad.
"Daniel's birthday cake looks good.
Thanks for making it, Gran."

In the afternoon
Dad looked after Daniel,
and Gran and Jessica
went shopping.

"It's Daniel's birthday
on Saturday," said Gran.
"Here's the toy shop."

13

Jessica looked
in the toy-shop window,
and she saw a rope ladder.
"Can we get it for Daniel?"
she said.

"Yes, let's get the rope ladder!"
said Gran.

On his birthday
Daniel said,
"Look at me!
Now I can
climb up to
the tree house
like Jessica!"